TABLE OF CONTENTS

INTRODUCTION

The time: Thursday, May 4, 1989. The place: Bartlett, Texas, 35 miles north of Austin.

Nine-year-old Derrick "Kye" Smith was visiting his grandparents' house while his mother worked as a nurse's aide. Kye was having a wonderful time studying baseball cards with his cousins. Kye loved baseball. He was a member of a midget-league baseball team and had already shown great talent for the game. This afternoon, no game or practice was scheduled. It was the perfect time to sort out his baseball cards, to see which ones he needed to complete different teams for his collection. Kye and his cousins were stacking the cards, separating out teams and player positions. They were so busy they didn't notice Kye's two-year-old brother.

Suddenly, one of Kye's cousins looked up. There, across the room, was Kye's little brother. In his hand was a gun...a real gun. A loaded gun. The little boy thought it was a toy. He had taken it out of a dresser drawer so he could play. Kye's cousin, also nine years old, knew that this was no toy. He quickly snatched it from the baby's hand.

The gun fired. Kye fell from the sofa. His baseball cards scattered all over the room. Kye had been struck by a bullet! The ambulance came quickly. But it was too late. Derrick "Kye" Smith, age nine, was dead on arrival at the hospital.

Why was Kye dead? He wasn't the victim of a crime. His death was a terrible accident. But many people believe this

Some people believe their relatives might be alive today if this country had passed laws controlling the sale of handguns.

accident would not have happened if guns were harder to get. They believe Kye would still be alive if this country had *gun control.*

WHAT IS GUN CONTROL?

Gun control means government control of what guns can be made or sold and who can buy them. We have very little gun control in the United States. When the United States was created more than 200 years ago, the *founding fathers* wrote the *Constitution,* outlining the laws that would govern the country. They realized that the people should be able to change the laws, so they made it possible to amend or change the Constitution.

On December 15, 1791, the first ten amendments were added to the Constitution. They became known as the Bill of Rights. The *Second Amendment* reads, "A well regulated Militia, being necessary to the security of a free State, the right of the people to keep and bear Arms, shall not be infringed." This means, according to some constitutional experts, that U.S. citizens who belong to a military group can buy and own guns and defend their property.

Early lawmakers thought this protection was necessary because of the restrictions the British had placed on the American colonists. They did not want American citizens to be defenseless against repressive government forces.

Today, many people believe this freedom has been

abused and that many people own guns for the wrong reasons.

Violence caused by firearms is increasing every year. Many people want to restrict the making, selling, transporting, and buying of guns. If guns are harder to get, they believe, we will have fewer gun-related deaths and injuries. They want gun control.

But other people feel that any restriction on getting a gun is against the constitutional amendment. They quote the Second Amendment: "the right of the people to keep and bear Arms, shall not be infringed." They believe that the founding fathers meant "every able-bodied man" and not a military group when they referred to "Militia," since that's how many other political documents of the time defined the term. The people against gun control often say guns do not kill people —*people* kill people. They argue that if these people can't get guns, they will use other weapons. People who favor gun control answer by pointing out that attacks with guns are far more likely to be fatal than attacks with other weapons.

Records show that a little more than 14 people in every 100,000 died of gunshot wounds in 1938. By 1980, that number had dropped to 13 people in every 100,000. But this was not because fewer people were getting shot. It was because hospital emergency rooms were getting better—more wounded people were being saved. Five times more people are wounded by guns than are killed by them.

But how are people killed by guns? Are they all killed by

criminals? Are they killed by *suicide?* Are they killed during an argument with someone they know? The answers to these questions may surprise you.

CRIME, ACCIDENTS, AND SUICIDES

The July 17, 1989, issue of *Time,* the weekly newsmagazine, reported all the gun deaths in a single, "average" week. All the facts about these deaths were examined. It was discovered that gun deaths happen in every state. They happen to every kind of person — rich, poor, young, old, male, female, black, white, Asian, Hispanic.

The magazine found that deaths by guns are caused most often by gun owners or people who know the gun owner well. Only 14 of the week's 464 deaths were in self-defense; only 13 involved policemen or other law enforcement agents.

It also noticed that most of the deaths were caused by ordinary *pistols* and not by sophisticated *assault weapons.*

Many people who favor gun control point to the danger from gun-carrying drug dealers and other criminals. They also explain that the average *homicide* is committed by someone the victim knows — a husband or wife, relative, or friend. What's more, 216 of the 464 people killed by guns during *Time* magazine's average week were

A boy at target practice with his pistol. Headphones protect his ears from the gun's blast.

suicides — people who shot themselves. Nine of these suicides killed other people before killing themselves.

Twenty-two of the 464 deaths studied were accidents. They could have been prevented had someone been more careful. Those in favor of gun control believe most of these accidental deaths would not have happened if guns were

Time *magazine reported that 464 people were killed by guns in one week in 1989; 216 of those deaths were suicides.*

harder to get. Those opposed to gun control feel that more education about gun safety, not fewer guns, is the answer.

The argument about gun control has been going on since before the United States government was formed. Even during the drafting of the Constitution, some delegates wanted to restrict private gun ownership. What events have caused the debate to become so heated today?

THE MODERN GUN CONTROL ARGUMENT

Many Americans have become more concerned about gun control since November 22, 1963, when President John F. Kennedy was *assassinated*. People asked, "Why is it so easy for just about anyone to get a gun?" Lee Harvey Oswald, the man believed to have shot Kennedy, did so with a rifle he bought through the mail.

Other assassinations and attempted assassinations of famous people have further fed interest in gun control.

• February 21, 1965: Black Muslim leader Malcolm X was shot and killed with a sawed-off shotgun.

• April 4, 1968: Civil rights leader Dr. Martin Luther King was assassinated by James Earl Ray in Memphis, Tennessee.

• June 5, 1968: President Kennedy's brother, New York Senator Robert F. Kennedy was shot by Sirhan B. Sirhan. Senator Kennedy died the next day.

• May 15, 1972: George Wallace, governor of Alabama and presidential hopeful, was wounded and left partially paralyzed by Arthur Bremer who used a .38 caliber revolver bought four months earlier.

• September 1975: President Gerald Ford escaped two assassination attempts. On September 5, Lynette "Squeaky" Fromme tried but failed to fire a .45 caliber pistol at him in Sacramento, California. Only 18 days later,

11

in San Francisco, Jane Moore did fire at the president. She missed because a former Marine in the crowd deflected her aim.

• December 8, 1980: John Lennon, singer, composer, political activist, and founding member of the Beatles rock group, was shot and killed outside his home in New York City.

• March 30, 1981: President Ronald Reagan was shot by John W. Hinckley while leaving a Washington hotel. Hinckley's shots also wounded three others, including presidential press secretary James Brady.

The assassination or attempted assassination of a famous person happens rarely compared to gun deaths of average citizens. But the publicity such cases receive calls more attention to the problem of guns. Such shattering events bring more attention to the debate over gun control, as well.

People who favor gun control say that these terrible murders and woundings would not happen if guns were harder to get. Those opposed say killers would just use different weapons. They say that laws to control the transport, selling, buying, and owning of guns deny rights. They say that the Second Amendment to the Constitution guarantees these rights to U.S. citizens.

Murders make newspaper headlines and the evening television news. But accidental deaths are also an important part of the debate. People for and against gun control have to consider the people who die each day because someone is careless.

Police roll a covered corpse out of a building.

ACCIDENTAL DEATHS

Justin Price was a 12-year-old resident of Morrison, Oklahoma, a small town 60 miles northeast of Oklahoma City. A typical American kid, Justin liked to play and

explore with his friends. On Saturday, May 6, 1989, such playing and exploring led Justin and a playmate into a garage. Garages are often filled with interesting objects. They can also be storage places for deadly things.

In this garage, Justin and his friend found a revolver. As his friend examined the gun in his hand, it fired, sending a bullet into Justin's face, killing him.

Justin Price, as well as Derrick "Kye" Smith, whose story began this book, are among almost 3,000 people in the United States who die from accidental gunshot wounds annually. These accidents sometimes occur while hunting, on farms, and in public places. But most gun accidents — 60 out of every 100 — happen at home. The victims of these accidents are mostly women and children.

Statistics also show that more guns mean more chance of accidental death. More people own guns in the South than anywhere else in the country. There, 2.46 accidental gun deaths happen per 100,000 guns owned. Compare this to 1.25 accidental deaths per 100,000 guns in the West and Midwest. Or just 0.59 per 100,000 guns in the North, the area of the country having the fewest private gun owners!

And deaths are only one part of the problem. Serious, permanent injuries caused by guns can extend the grief of a gun accident for a lifetime. A 1975 report showed that 183,000 gun accidents occur each year. This was 80 percent more than in 1968. Four of every 100 adults questioned in a 1978 survey had been involved in a gun accident. Ten out of 100 said that a family member had had a gun accident; 15 out of 100 said a friend had.

A fourteen-year-old hunter takes aim at his prey with a rifle. There are four times as many deaths from accidents in areas where owning a gun is common.

Everyone agrees that guns are dangerous. People disagree on how to handle the danger. Some people say, "Get rid of the guns." Others say, "Learn to handle them safely." These people also point out that guns cause fewer accidental deaths than car crashes, falls, drownings, burns, or poisonings. Guns are the sixth major cause of accidental deaths.

This pistol from the Old West is a collector's item. Many collectors keep handguns like this at home.

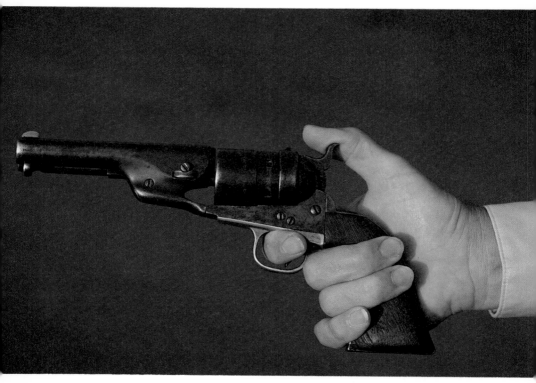

Since most people keep their guns at home, you can understand why more deaths happen there. But today, guns are showing up in places where they were once never found.

GUNS IN SCHOOL

Early one morning, four workmen were assembling something strange in the doorway of a New York City school. It looked like a phone booth without glass. Many students watched and wondered what the strange device was. But a senior who had just come back from a vacation with his parents recognized it instantly. "It's a metal detector," he said, "just like they use at the airports!"

He was right. In 1989, *metal detectors* were put in five New York City schools located in high crime areas. Their purpose: to prevent students from bringing guns into school. Official records show that the problem of guns in schools is growing, even as other types of in-school problems decrease.

In the New York City schools, 1,400 incidents with guns happened during the 1986-87 school year. That number rose to 1,916 in 1987-88.

Guns in schools are a growing problem throughout the country, not just in cities such as New York, Los Angeles

A policeman searches for guns with a portable metal detector at a rally in Texas.

and Philadelphia. In Florida, some public schools have a "Say No to Guns" program. This began after 17 teenagers in one county died from gunshot wounds in a single year. In Baltimore, three children were shot at a football game. In Detroit, police make spot checks with a portable metal detector. They have a hotline kids can call if they have information about someone with a gun.

The reasons kids bring guns to school are many. Some don't know the guns are real and bring them just to show their friends. Others take guns to school to scare other students or even teachers. In response, other students carry weapons in self-defense.

Schools are trying many methods to stop students from bringing guns to class. The metal detectors are one way. Another is teaching gun safety.

The *National Rifle Association (NRA)* feels that many of the programs taught in school about the gun problem are anti-gun. They have written their own program featuring a comic character, Eddie the Eagle, who teaches kids gun safety.

Beefed-up security is another response to guns in schools. However, some school officials believe the problem is not school security but the ease with which students can get guns.

Guns in schools contribute to the number of people who are killed or hurt in this country. But the greatest number of gun deaths and injuries comes from criminals and guns in criminal hands.

CRIME

It was Wednesday, May 3, 1989, in San Antonio, Texas. Ten police patrolmen cautiously approached a house. The police had suspected for a long time that the house was the hideout of drug dealers. With them, they had a *search warrant* that would allow them to look through the house for illegal drugs. Patrolman Raymond Phillips kicked open the front door, hoping to surprise any of the suspected drug dealers who might be hiding inside. But Owen Hazen, the man inside the house, was ready. As soon as Phillips broke in, Hazen fired a 12-gauge shotgun right at the officer's chest. Phillips was thrown back by the force of the blast, but survived, saved by a bulletproof vest. Instantly, Phillips returned the fire with his .357 Magnum revolver, killing Hazen. Near Hazen's body another 12-gauge shotgun was found. It was loaded and ready to fire.

Just as people don't agree about gun control, they don't always agree about what causes crime. Nevertheless, there is no disagreement about this: criminals use guns to commit every variety of crime.

Statistics show that 64 out of 100 violent crimes in America involve *handguns.* Gun control supporters say that making guns hard or impossible to get will reduce these crimes. People against gun control say that criminals will simply use different weapons. They also say that controls do not work. In 1968, Congress passed the Gun Control Act to stop people from importing cheap handguns into the United States. Since the law passed, say those against gun control, the number of homicides caused by guns in the United States has risen 300 percent! The Act named only certain guns, and imports of these guns did lessen. But the import of other types of guns, not specifically mentioned in the Act, increased.

Texas County police perfect their skill with handguns at target practice.

Those against gun control say that armed citizens will make criminals think twice about robbing or attacking innocent people. Those for control wonder if this is true.

DETERRENT TO CRIMINALS

In Gardena, California, Steve Koo operated a local convenience store. Fearful of criminals who might rob the

This blunt sign at a Christmas tree farm is meant to keep thieves and trespassers away. But no one knows whether the threat of guns really scares criminals.

store, Koo kept a gun behind the counter. Although he didn't want to use the gun, he would if he had to. Then, on May 1, 1989, the terrible time came. Leonard Williams entered Koo's store, gun in hand, to rob the place. Quickly, Koo pulled out his gun to defend his store and his livelihood. Both men fired. Hit, Williams staggered to the store's parking lot and fell dead. Koo's gun had done its job.

The robbery was prevented, and Leonard Williams would never rob another store again. But the price was high. Williams's bullet had struck Koo, and he died the next day.

Guns kept in small stores or even in the home may discourage criminals, but it is difficult to know for sure. Opinion polls show that every other household in the United States has a gun. The only way to see if these weapons do keep criminals away would be to remove the guns and wait to see if the crime rate goes up. Nevertheless, people who own guns in their homes or businesses "for protection" say they feel safer. They do not worry as much about criminals entering or breaking into their homes or stores.

Unfortunately, statistics show that guns in the home, if ever fired, are usually fired at members of the household, not at burglars. Some of these shootings are accidents. But nearby guns can also turn family arguments into murder. In Detroit, Michigan, for instance, more people were killed in one year by home gun accidents than in four and a half years by robbers or burglars.

EXISTING GUN CONTROL LAWS

Although debate about gun control continues, the United States already has some 20,000 laws on the books about guns. That's more than in any other country in the world.

The earliest laws about guns in the United States went on the books even before the Revolutionary War. The Massachusetts Colony passed a law prohibiting carrying weapons in public places. In the 1800s, states, including Kentucky, Indiana, Arkansas, and Georgia, passed laws

A young boy learning how to fire a rifle

making it a crime to carry a *concealed weapon*. Today, 49 states have such laws. New Mexico is the only exception.

These laws did not restrict anyone's right to buy or own a gun. They did control when, where, and how people could use their guns. Such laws are called *place and manner laws*. Most of the nation's large cities, and the 49 states mentioned earlier, have place and manner laws about guns.

Twenty-one states require everyone to have a special license to carry a gun in a car. The Massachusetts law is very strict about this. Anyone caught carrying a gun in his or her car without a license gets a *mandatory sentence* of one year in jail. That means they have to go to jail for a year. No ifs, ands, or buts. And no *parole*.

Until 1972, people could easily get guns through the U.S. mail. In this way, many people got around state laws about gun sales since the mails are run by the U.S. government. Gun control *advocates* successfully eliminated much of this by lobbying for federal laws restricting many mail-order gun sales.

GUN CONTROLS IN OTHER COUNTRIES

In 1968, the U.S. State Department asked its diplomats for information on local gun control regulations in 102 countries.

They found that 29 European countries have laws that require citizens either to have a license to carry guns or to register their guns. Five countries prohibit private ownership of guns altogether.

In addition to the United States, fifteen countries in North and South America require licensing and registration of guns. In Mexico, these laws are local, not national. El Salvador has no restrictions except inside city limits. Nicaraguans may own guns, but they must follow laws about how and where to carry them. Paraguay has no laws about guns at all.

All 21 Asian countries surveyed reported license and registration laws. In the Soviet Union, anyone who has a hunting license can own a smooth-bore hunting gun. Australia and New Zealand have no restrictions on sporting guns. Afghanistan and Japan have outlawed handguns completely.

In Africa, 25 out of 33 countries questioned have laws that require people to register guns they buy or sell. The others have laws relating to owning and carrying guns. Three African countries prohibit handguns completely; in four, no one can own a military weapon. In Algeria, you have to belong to a sporting club to own a sporting gun.

Supporters and opponents of gun control in the United States use these foreign gun control laws to uphold their own views. For instance, supporters point to England as an example of good gun control. The restrictions against private gun ownership are heavy there, and it is very difficult for anyone to obtain a gun. Only 18 out of any 100 homicides in England are committed with a gun. In the United States, 64 out of 100 are. Only 6 of every 100 robbers in England use guns, while 36 out of 100 in the United States do. Gun control supporters say that these statistics show the success of tough gun control laws. Detractors say they show only that criminals will switch weapons if they can't find guns. They say that the crime rate won't drop if gun controls are imposed. The statistics appear to prove this. There is little difference in the urban crime rate in England as compared to the United States.

The difficulty that supporters of gun control face in the United States is that the "right to bear arms" is part of the very laws that created our country.

A British Bobby talks with a driver in London, where police do not carry guns.

THE "RIGHT TO BEAR ARMS"

Interpretation of the Second Amendment is what separates pro- and anti-gun control groups.

The National Rifle Association (NRA) has the phrase "The right of the people to keep and bear Arms, shall not be infringed" carved in the front of its Washington, D.C., headquarters. Gun control advocates claim that the NRA omits the first part of the amendment on purpose. They say that the phrase "well regulated Militia" refers to something like the National Guard, and not to individuals.

To counter these claims, the NRA and other anti-gun control groups have studied American history and found cases that support their argument. Just prior to the American Revolution, the British took away citizens' weapons in Boston. The "shot heard 'round the world," the first shot of the American Revolution, was fired to stop the Redcoats from taking the Minutemen's *arsenal*. The right to own firearms was very important to the founding fathers.

George Mason, debating before the Virginia Assembly on June 16, 1788, stated that "militia" referred to "the whole of the people." Mason was a Virginia statesman who helped draft the Constitution. Thomas Jefferson also said that the militia was "every man able to bear arms." In his *Federalist Papers,* James Madison referred to "a militia of near half a million men." Since the 1790 population numbered only about 800,000 free men, anti-gun control groups argue that he was referring to "every able-bodied man."

Different interpretations of the Constitution (on all issues, not just the Second Amendment) are discussed constantly. There will probably never be one, single, universally accepted interpretation of this document. That people can decipher it differently and debate their ideas is one of the things that makes the United States a free country.

Nevertheless, some people believe that the debate over gun control may result in restrictions of their basic American freedoms.

A road sign in Illinois suggests how strongly Americans feel about the Second Amendment. The author of this sign feels that guns prove a person has courage and loves God.

HUNTING

The farmer crouched low behind his stalks of corn. He aimed his rifle carefully. Through the telescopic sight he could see the deer at the edge of his field. For the past week he had seen signs of foraging in his corn crop. Deer, starving because of the lack of food in the forest, had begun to eat his crops and destroy his fences. Now, there was only one thing left to do.

As the deer crossed into the field, the farmer fired. One deer fell dead, and the others ran through the forest away from his field. The farmer's gun had not only stopped the destruction of his crops, but it had also provided his family with deer meat for the winter.

One of the main reasons people list for owning a gun is hunting. Hunters defend their sport by pointing to the environmental and crop damage some animals do. Along the same lines, they argue that because the growth of cities and towns has reduced the wilderness, many animals simply starve in the wild. Seasonal hunting reduces the herds and allows for a better natural balance between animals and nature, they say.

Animal rights supporters tend to disagree with this argument. Today, few people hunt because they need food, they say. Most food animals are raised and killed under controlled conditions on farms or game reserves.

Many hunters fear that gun control will deny them the right to hunt. Others who oppose gun control fear that

Hunters waiting for ducks in a blind built of reeds in a salt marsh

Hunters like these fear that gun control laws will curtail their right to stalk ducks and deer for sport.

forced registration of guns will be the first step toward the eventual seizure of all guns by a government agency. Gun control supporters say that they do not want the seizure of all guns. They just want to make it impossible or extremely difficult for criminals to get guns. They also want to make guns designed specifically to kill people, such as most handguns, illegal. "Rifles and shotguns," say gun control advocates, "are not part of the problem." Even so, gun owners feel that regulations regarding handguns will be interpreted by some to include restrictions on their sport and against their right to defend their property.

SELF-DEFENSE

Many people own handguns. They are the most popular weapon among criminals. They are also the most popular weapon for self-defense. In fact, when asked why they own a gun, 71 of 100 people answer, "for self-defense."

People against gun control argue that criminals won't attack people they know can handle a gun. Gun control advocates counter that gun owners who do fire their weapons usually harm themselves or loved ones.

The anti-gun control side cites a 1966-67 Orlando, Florida, program to support its argument. That program trained women to use firearms for self-defense. During the months classes were conducted, the crime rate fell. Orlando was the only large American city to show a decrease in its crime rate that year.

Sport shooters like this boy take aim at artificial targets. Marksmanship is the chief object of the sport for them.

Gun control opponents also point to New York City. Its gun control laws are so strict that it's almost impossible for a private citizen to own a gun legally. At the same time, the city has the highest robbery rate in the country.

The gun control supporters agree that training private citizens in the use of guns helps. But they point out that most people are not trained. Statistics show that the average citizen owning a gun is six times more likely to shoot an innocent person than a criminal. For every burglar stopped by a handgun, four members of gun-owning families have been killed in gun accidents.

Also, 90 out of 100 break-ins happen when no one is home, and guns are one of the most popular items to steal. About 100,000 handguns are stolen each year.

AGAINST GUN CONTROL

The most famous and powerful group opposed to gun control is the National Rifle Association, better known as the NRA. The NRA was founded in 1871 by officers of the National Guard. They founded the group because they had seen poor marksmanship in the military forces of the day. They wanted to set an example of good, accurate, and safe gun ownership. The NRA is the oldest sportsmen's organization in the country. The membership is made up of gun collectors, gun dealers, gun manufacturers, hunters, and *sports shooters*. The group has over one million members.

The National Rifle Association was begun to teach safe marksmanship to men who would one day be soldiers.

The NRA spends a great deal of time promoting good marksmanship. It holds shooting competitions all around the country. It also has training programs for hunters. NRA members believe that many gun control laws restrict the rights of Americans to own guns for lawful purposes. From its offices in Washington, D.C., the NRA works against gun control. Its officers speak to citizens' groups and elected officials to convince them of their position.

In its publication, *The American Rifleman,* the NRA reports on any laws or proposals on gun control. It urges its members to write their representatives in Congress to tell them to vote against gun control laws. It also maintains the NRA Political Victory Fund, which gives money to candidates who agree with the NRA's anti-gun control position.

FOR GUN CONTROL

Organized groups in favor of gun control are many, but they are smaller than the NRA. Many were founded after gun-related tragedies. For instance, Handgun Control, Inc., was founded by Nelson T. "Pete" Shields III, a former executive with the DuPont Company. His 23-year-old son, Nick Shields, was killed in 1974. Nick Shields was a victim of the "Zebra" killings in San Francisco, California. The "Zebra" murders were senseless, brutal killings named for a special police radio band reserved for reports of these murders. The "Zebra Killer" was never apprehended.

Handgun Control, Inc., is a *lobby* for handgun control. Its Washington, D.C., office keeps a thorough file of articles, research, statistics, and laws on gun control. Today's vice-chairperson of Handgun Control, Inc., is Sarah Brady. She has this job because of a tragedy that shocked the world.

On March 30, 1981, President Ronald Reagan left the Washington Hilton Hotel after giving a speech. He was surrounded by Secret Service agents. Washington police and James Brady, his press secretary, were there, too. The president made his way from a back door of the hotel to his limousine. A small crowd had gathered to see him.

Suddenly, four shots rang out from the middle of the crowd. Twenty-five-year-old John W. Hinckley had fired at the president. In seconds, police and Secret Service agents wrestled Hinckley to the ground. But the damage was done. President Reagan, James Brady, and two others had been hit. The president was hit in the lung and soon recovered. But Press Secretary Brady had been shot in the head. At one point, he was actually reported dead.

After many operations, and with support from his family, friends, and the President, Brady made a spectacular recovery, although he will never be 100 percent well again. His strongest supporter was his wife. Since the shooting, Sarah Brady has become a powerful political activist for gun control in the United States.

Prior to her husband's injury, Sarah Brady was active politically, working for the Republican Party. But as the wife of the president's press secretary, she didn't catch the public's eye very much. When her husband was shot, she

James Brady (in blue pants) and patrolman Delaney (foreground) shortly after they were shot by John Hinckley.

started to speak out more forcefully for the issues she believed in. Her strong efforts on behalf of her husband drew public attention. As more people listened, she drew more attention to gun control. As vice-chairperson of Handgun Control, Inc., she led the fight in Maryland to uphold a ban on the *Saturday night special*, a cheap, short-barreled gun extremely popular with criminals. Even though the NRA spent over $5 million on a campaign to get rid of the law, voters were behind Sarah Brady. The law is still in effect.

Today, she is working on the Brady Amendment. This law would require a waiting period between the time someone applies to buy a gun and the time the application is approved. This would allow time to check out the buyer to make sure he or she does not have a criminal background. It would be a national law.

Sarah Brady supported an earlier version of this bill. Many groups joined her — Republicans and Democrats, liberals and conservatives. The bill failed to pass by 24 votes. But she is working hard for a victory next time around.

Other groups were born out of other incidents and needs. The National Council for the Control of Handguns (NCCH) was founded by Mark Borinsky. He was robbed and almost killed at gunpoint when he was a graduate student at the University of Chicago. Borinsky and a friend were jumped by three men while they were walking back to campus. One of the men kept urging, "Let's shoot 'em!" Luckily, the other attackers didn't listen. Borinsky and his friend lost only some money and their shoes. The criminals took the shoes so that they would not be followed. When Borinsky went to Washington some time later, he wanted to join a gun control lobby. He wanted to help the cause of gun control. At the time, Borinsky found no effective organization. He founded his own: the NCCH.

Yet another group is the National Coalition to Ban Handguns. It was founded by several smaller gun control groups. They wanted a more powerful voice in Washington. This group conducts workshops and provides consulting and referral services on gun control.

GUN CONTROL— ARE THERE ANSWERS?

The question of gun control — should or shouldn't we have it? — may never be completely answered. As time goes by, opinions in our country change. Each new generation has different ideas about issues because the world changes and technology changes. Every generation faces problems its parents and grandparents never imagined.

Advances in weapons may someday make strict gun control necessary. Advances in law enforcement may make such laws unnecessary. Future discoveries may make firearms obsolete. No one knows. No one can predict the

A gun control advocate's idea of what arms are for

future of the gun control question. All each person can do is learn about both sides of the issue, then make a decision.

Do you support gun control? Are you against it? Only you can decide. Once you do, support your position as best you can.

FOR MORE INFORMATION

For more information about gun control, write to:

Handgun Control, Inc.
1400 K Street, NW
Suite 500
Washington, DC 20005

National Council for a Responsible
Firearms Policy
7216 Stafford Road
Alexandria, VA 22037

National Association to Keep and Bear Arms
P.O. Box 78336
8434 Rainer Avenue, S
Seattle, Washington 98178

National Coalition to Ban Handguns
100 Maryland Avenue, NW
Washington, DC 20002

National Rifle Association
311 First Street, NW
Washington, DC 20001

Police Foundation/Communications Office
1001 22nd Street, NW
Suite 200
Washington, DC 20037

GLOSSARY/INDEX

ADVOCATE — *A person who speaks or writes in favor of a particular cause or goal.* 25, 35

ARSENAL — *A collection of weapons. Also a storage place for weapons.* 28

ASSASSINATED — *Killed by secret or surprise, usually for political rather than personal reasons.* 11, 12

ASSAULT WEAPONS — *Guns designed especially for military attack rather than self-defense.* 8

CONCEALED WEAPON — *Any weapon hidden on a person so a casual observer can't see it.* 25

CONSTITUTION — *The document describing the fundamental laws of the United States. It was framed and adopted in 1788 and put into effect March 4, 1789.* 6, 7, 11, 12, 28, 29

FEDERALIST PAPERS — *A collection of essays published in 1787 and 1788 to refute arguments opposing the Constitution. Many were written by James Madison.* 28

FOUNDING FATHERS — *The men who organized our form of government, created our first laws, and composed, wrote, and signed the Declaration of Independence and the Constitution. George Washington, Benjamin Franklin, Thomas Jefferson, James Madison, and their contemporaries were our founding fathers.* 6, 7, 28

GUN CONTROL — *Laws restricting the manufacture, sale, transport, and ownership of firearms by the general public.* 6, 7, 10, 11, 12, 13, 20, 21, 23, 25, 26, 27, 28, 29, 31, 35, 36, 38, 39, 42, 43, 44

46

GLOSSARY/INDEX

47

GLOSSARY/INDEX

SATURDAY NIGHT SPECIAL — *A cheap, short-barreled, low-caliber gun extremely popular with criminals. 41*

SEARCH WARRANT — *A written order issued by legal authority to inspect private premises for the purpose of making an arrest or obtaining evidence of a crime. Search warrants are not issued unless law enforcement agents can show that they have good reasons for suspecting the premises are the hiding place of a criminal or evidence. 20*

SECOND AMENDMENT — *One of the Bill of Rights, added to the Constitution in 1791, which reads: "A well regulated Militia, being necessary to the security of a free State, the right of the people to keep and bear Arms, shall not be infringed." 6, 7, 12, 28, 29*

SPORTS SHOOTERS — *People who use guns for fun, as in hunting or target practice. 36*

SUICIDE — *The taking of one's own life. 8, 9*